D1498785

1. *Sayings of Jeanne Jugan*

Sayings of Jeanne Jugan

FOUNDRESS OF THE LITTLE SISTERS OF THE POOR

Neither her biography nor her spiritual journey, but, contained in her sayings, something of the soul of "Sister Mary of the Cross".

NIHIL OBSTAT: T. VEECH, Cens. Dep.

IMPRIMATUR: Sydney, 30th June, 1970

JAMES MADDEN, Vic. Gen.

PROLOGUE

God has foreseen everything,

Our destinies

And the circumstances that influence our lives:

The times in which we live, our family,

Our social environment,

Certain gifts of intelligence, certain aptitudes.

Let us not be astonished if, from the very

                                beginning,

Some seem more favoured than others;
More intelligent, better developed, better gifted.
These are just deceptive appearances.
God does not see things in this way.
He knows that all the clay coming from his hands
Is good for making Saints.

Whether the clay is more or less of inferior
                                        quality,
Is his affair,
Not ours.
All he asks of us
Is to be clearsighted,
And to take others (and ourselves),
Just as he made them.

In any life, it is never just the natural gifts
That are admirable,
It is the beauty the clay takes
In the hands of the Divine Potter.

There we have the whole story of Jeanne Jugan.

To begin with,

Very little:
A turbulent period (She was born in 1792) ;
A family of little importance;
Which was reduced to want following the
                              disappearance of the Father,
Who was a sailor, as are almost all the men of
                                        Cancale.
The child just learns to read and to write
—And that's already something—

As a young girl, she is placed "in service".
When she is past forty,
She is still serving in other people's homes
And there is no reason why this should change.
Yet, somehow, yes . . .

One day, everything is changed.
The desire of the religious life, dwelling within
                              her these past twenty years,
Becomes a reality. At last!
She who has always obeyed,
Directs,
Organises,
Gives orders,
Founds Homes, saves them from shipwreck.

One would think that she had never done
                                    anything else
Throughout her whole life.

But yet a little while . . .
Another task awaits her, a greater one:

To suffer, to be silent, and once again to obey.
And, by doing this, to engrave deeply
The imprint of her soul
On the religious family she has founded.

Only a few years of activity,
Few words,
No writings.
A great work.
A masterpiece for God.

Certain sayings of Jeanne Jugan
Struck so forcibly those who heard them
That they have been handed down even to us,
Just as they came from her lips,

Quite up to date, in spite of a form which is
                        sometimes old-fashioned.
Stripped of the merely human,
Bearers of a message that is ever new.

If they had come from other lips, one would
                        say: banale,
Commonplace.
On Jeanne's lips, they strike us.
They reach direct
To the best that is in us.
Like the lowly sermons
Of a Cure of Ars.
We see that they come from the depths
Of a soul.
Of a soul very close to God.

Do not delay, I beg you, over the commentary.
It explains nothing.
It adds nothing.
It is a little like the plaster figures of our cribs.
At first they attract all our attention,
They take up all the room.
But, really, they are of no importance.

They are only there to draw our gaze
From the girl with the lavender, to the shepherd,
From the boy with the horn, to the peasant,
Towards the tiny Jesus,
Who takes up much less space than them all
And yet is the only One who really counts
At the crib.

So it is for the words of Jeanne Jugan,
They alone count in these pages.
They alone have something to say to you.
If you put aside the commentary altogether,
So much the better.
It will have attained its end.

"God wants me for Himself.
He is keeping me for a work
as yet unknown, for a work
which is not yet founded . . ."

"Do not call me Jeanne Jugan.
All that is left of her is Sister
Mary of the Cross—unworthy
though she is of that lovely
name."

Fait et délibéré par la Supérieure Gé...

en la Maison - Mère de Rennes le 19 ...

Sr marie au...

Supre gé...

Sr Marie de la Conception

et Gle   Sr Stéphanie

Sr Marie gertrude,   pse de...

Sr Marie de la croix Sr Lucie = Marie

J'espère qu'être extérieurement édifié de...

She left us no spiritual writings,
No manuscript, no letters,
Nothing.

Nothing except her signature,
On an official document, one amongst many.
The others are fine signatures
—Signatures of people who are aware that they
                                    know how to write.

◄ Document bearing the signature of Sister Mary of the Cross.

And to write well—
With flourishes,
Studied lettering,
Elegant,
Complicated.

That of Sister Mary of the Cross is altogether
                                    different,
Neither learned nor clever,
—Evidently she didn't make frequent use of the
                                    pen—
But how revealing:
Simple, true, without affectation,
Sincere, with the sincerity of a soul who has
        never sought to appear more than she was.
And at the same time,
Without knowing it,
She reveals her soul to us.

Why should we regret having no other writings
Of Jeanne Jugan?
Does not her signature tell us
All that she has to hand down to us?

And to teach us?

Mary of the Cross.
Her name.

Doubtless, it was of her own choosing.
It was probably the last thing she chose.
From then on she would no longer choose;
She would allow God to arrange things as He
                                        pleased.

Already, in fact, He had begun to arrange them.
He had placed her in the shadows.
She could, in all truth, choose to be called
Mary of the Cross.

However, it was only the beginning;
Thirty-five years,—the remaining years of her
                                        life—
Would not be too many to make of it the very
                                        life of her life,
To identify herself with it,
To become in all truth
Mary of the Cross.

Mary.
An "Ecce" ever renewed,

A "Fiat" into which flowed all the love of her
                                     soul,
A "Magnificat" as clear and joyous as the song of
                                     a child.

And all things "kept in her heart" . . .
An ordinary life, so very ordinary;
You couldn't imagine more ordinary tasks.
But God at the heart of everything,
At the centre of everything.

A life where all is for God,
Where all is of God,
Where one "no longer sees anything but God"
(She herself would say this one day).

With the Cross the focal point,
Because it cannot be otherwise.
Mary was, and was the first to be,
Bound to the mystery of the Cross, indissolubly.
And we, the same.

It is a question of love.
When one loves, thirty-five years is not too long
To strengthen such bonds,
And to remain there, standing;

Silently,
Without drawing attention,
Simply,
Simply because one loves.
United to Him who is Love,
A helper, like unto Him,
No longer knowing anything but Him,
Hidden, now, in Him.

"Give, give us the house;
if God fills it,
God will not abandon it."

"IF GOD IS WITH US, IT WILL BE ACCOMPLISHED . . ."

"Sister, that's foolishness!"

We would have applauded heartily.
The wife of the Sub-Prefect was perfectly right.
She was, without doubt, a good Christian,
Saying her prayers every morning:
"Let us place ourselves in the presence of God . . .
"My God, I firmly believe . . .

"My God, I hope with a firm confidence . . ."

But, all the same, one should hope for reasonable
things,
And not be like
This old maid Jeanne Jugan
Who hasn't a cent to her name
And comes to speak to you about opening a
Home,

To take in the poor,
To care for them,
To feed them . . .
But with what?
Come, come now . . .
"Sister, that's foolishness!"

We would have said the very same thing.
The most difficult thing to understand about
God's Friends
Is not their zeal for souls,
Their forgetfulness of self,
Their love of prayer.

The most difficult thing
Is the way they look to God for support.

This statuette of St. Joseph was, with her Rosary, the only pious object belonging to Sister Mary of the Cross. Given by her, in 1873, to a benefactor, the statuette was given back to the Congregation encased in a golden container.

Not capriciously, to satisfy their every whim,
Or to obtain all that they want,
But in order to undertake things which astound

us,

And to press forward against wind and tide,
And to succeed
Just where we thought they were going to fail.

Listen to Jeanne reply,
Calmly,
Quietly,
Decidedly:
"If God is with us, it will be accomplished!"

Not a shadow of susceptibility.
Why should she have been offended
To have anyone say to her, "That's foolishness!"?
She knows that already.
It's not a new idea.
Saint Paul said it before you did, my dear lady.

And today still,
We are continually tempted to repeat it
Whenever it is given us to meet

One of your true Friends,
Lord.
One of those who can say,
As though it were the simplest thing in the world:
"If God is with us, it will be accomplished."

To cultivate such a friendship with You,
And to rely on You
To that extent,
Is not a common occurrence.
As for us, Lord, we confuse our projects with

                                        Yours.
With your Friends, it is just the opposite.

With Jeanne, there is no question
Of calling "on God's help".
She doesn't imagine that He is going to help her
Accomplish her projects,
Her, Jeanne Jugan's, little plans.

She claims that the Lord will aid her
—Miserable creature that she is—
To accomplish His projects,

His,—God's.
His great divine projects.
A thousand times over and above the human
                                    possibilities of Jeanne.
God will lend her His own strength to do it.

She will do what she can,
He will do the rest.
But, whenever God lends His strength to His
                                    Friends,
He does not change them, for all that,
They remain just as they are.

Poor Jeanne!
More than others, she is aware of her
                                    deficiencies.
The same gaze which enables her to penetrate
                into the intentions of the Loved One
—Mystery of friendship—
That same gaze shows her that the task is
                                    altogether beyond her;
How easy it would be to shirk it!

"Lord, look for someone better educated than I,
Someone who is eloquent,
And who will be worthy of your choice.
As for me, well, I'm just not up to standard.

Lord, it's impossible, it's foolishness!"

Jeanne did not turn away,
The true Friends of God do not turn away.
No, Jeanne had discarded
All that was only of herself.

Her confidence no longer reposed in herself.
Her confidence was "in good hands".
From now on, she took refuge
In the hands of the "Master of the impossible".
At all times, in spite of all,
She could go forward.
All would end well.

God's affairs always end well,
When we don't place any obstacles in the way,
By our failings,
By refusing to co-operate,
By viewing things from a human standpoint only.

As for Jeanne, she adheres totally.
Docile. Supple.

Her response is always the one God is expecting.
Because she never deceives Him.
Because—setting self aside completely—
She enters, without a backward glance,
Without the slightest hesitation,
Into His divine designs,
God does not deceive her, either.
All does end well.

During her life—every time—
Everything that God had asked of her had ended

well.

One day—sooner or later—
She would be able to repeat
For herself alone,
In wonderment:

"It's true, it was foolishness,
"It appeared impossible,
"But God was with us."

"LITTLE ... VERY LITTLE ..."

The gardener watched her disappear,
She whom they still called
"The tall Jugan".
A real Cancalaise.
People often talked about her, for she had
                                        founded a work;
Many admired it,
Some were running it down. That's human
                                        nature.

They said she was the Superior;

That's not surprising: the women of Cancale are
*   past masters in the art of taking charge.*
And proud of it!

The gardener was musing on these thoughts,
Whilst in his mind's eye he could still see the
*   scene he had just witnessed:*
She, "the tall Jugan"

Who held out her basket for him to fill with
*   vegetables;*

Himself, suddenly ill at ease,
—For she was much more religious
Than you or me—
Asking awkwardly,
"Jeanne,
"What should we call you now?"

Simply, without fuss, came the retort,

"The humble servant of the poor".
A quick response,
Rising from the depths of her being;
It was as though she had given a definition of
*   herself,*

In all sincerity.

"The humble servant of the poor".
That she was.
She would be only that for the years to come.
No more than that.
But all of that.
"The humble servant of the poor".

Not a common ambition, but a magnificent one.
The same ambition as He
Whose voice she heard within her soul.
He said to her,
"Learn of me: I am gentle and humble of heart."
"I came not to be served, but to serve."

You learnt well, Sister Mary of the Cross.
The language of your Lord found a mysterious
                              preharmony in you.
Those same words
Contained your whole vocation,
And you would have to live them so well

"They'll talk to you about me . . .
Don't pay any attention. Our
good Lord knows the whole
story."

That you would draw many souls along the same
path.

For God willed you to be head of an army:
The first, and so the most humble,
The most humiliated as well.
True humility. Not just resignation.

A humility which in all things was like that of
your Master,
Which would make you available,
Docile to the divine will.
Yesterday at the summit, without vainglory.
Today downgraded, without bitterness.
An instrument.
A good instrument of redemption.

You wanted to become like this.
Humble, humiliated.
For you would resemble a little, from afar,
—But resemble, all the same—
Your humble Lord,
Your humiliated Lord.
Together with Him,
You would counterbalance

◀ A bronze, by E. Thiollier: Jeanne Jugan on the quest.

The world's pride.

We shall never know the depths
Humility reached in you.
We only know that you could not keep it secret.

On your lips, the same words keep returning,
                                    untiringly:
"Little . . . very little,
"Be very little before God."

"Remain little . . . hidden by humility,
"In all God wants from you,
"As being only the instruments of His work."

"If you keep the spirit of humility,
"Of simplicity,
"Of littleness . . ."

—What will happen, Sister Mary of the Cross,
                                    tell us?—

"My little ones . . .
"You will glorify God,

"You will obtain the conversion of souls!"

For the price of our littleness:
The glory of God,
The salvation of souls.
How great is the littleness that can buy such
                                        treasures!

How great you are, Sister Mary of the Cross!
Magnanimous,
And far from our human "pettiness";
Our "small minds", "little nothings",
The "tiny pinpricks" of life, which make **us**
                                        shudder.

Did such pettiness never touch you, then?
Touched you, perhaps, but took hold of you
                                        never!

Your "littleness" was hungry for greatness.
But of one kind only,
The one, the unique greatness:
God.
He, all,

You, nothing.

Little by little,
He so perfectly became your "all",
You so perfectly became his "nothing",
Little . . . very little,
That He placed in you a great spirit,
Seeing far and clear;
A great heart, without limits in its gift of self,
In openness to others.

The more we gaze at you, Sister Mary of the
                                        Cross,
The greater we see you to be.

Humiliation sounded the measure of your
                                        greatness.
Humiliated, we show just what we are,
With our hidden pettiness,
Our secret meanness.
No longer any chance of pretence: it is quite
                                        evident,
Uncovered in broad daylight.

For you too, humiliation was a revelation.
First of all, of your greatness;

But that was not enough.

Slowly,
Humiliation shaded both your features and
                                    your greatness.

And others features appeared,
Another greatness,
Divine Features.
Of Him who is gentle,
Who is humble,
Who was humiliated.

"IT IS SO GOOD TO BE POOR . . ."

You did not escape from the common way of

mortals:

On the threshold of old age
We feel the need of assuring our security,
To look ahead,
To take precautions for
"Our old age", as we say.

You did not escape from the common way of

mortals,

Sister Mary of the Cross.
You looked ahead:
A modest dwelling, but a well chosen one,
—A few steps from the Church—
A well-liked companion.
You calculated what you would be able to save:
A few more years of toil,
And then, a peaceful life.

At that moment,
You could not have said to us:
"My little ones, it is so good to be poor,
"To have nothing,
"To depend on God for everything."

He had not yet introduced you
To all the dimensions
Of the first Beatitude:
"Its height, its breadth, its depth",
In all its exigencies,
And the self-despoilment
That it imposes on those who embrace it.
A despoilment to which the simple experience
                              of material poverty
Cannot be compared.

"We were grafted onto the Cross."

Crucifix of profession of Sister Mary of the Cross discovered at her
exhumation, in 1936.

In that sphere you had nothing to learn.
You had always known it,
And its consequences:
Subjection to work,
Dependence on others, exacting, humiliating;
Privations, annoyances,
Insecurity.

You were then half way
Towards the first Beatitude.

There remained for you now to set out
On the second part of the journey,
That part where no one may enter alone,
Nor of his own accord,
But only on the divine invitation.

That invitation
Was heard by you,
Sister Mary of the Cross.
And you have known spiritual poverty,
The fullness of the first Beatitude,

The silence of a being,
In its native poverty.

"My little ones,
"It is so good to be poor,
"To have nothing,
"To depend on God for everything."

When you spoke thus,
At the end of your life,
What did you have left, humanly speaking?
Your liberty? Alienated.
Your work? Attributed to others.
Your reputation? Smothered.
You no longer had anything,
Anything at all.
You counted for nothing, nobody cared.
Forgotten,
Unknown,
Solitary.
"A nonentity on the earth".
Poor.

And you used to say:
"My little ones, it is so good!"
Yes, it is a Beatitude. The first.

"Blessed are the poor."
We—perhaps—would prefer to water down,
Not to take at its face value,
This astonishing statement.
Our selfishness is unwilling to understand.
Those only understand
Who, in the depths of their heart, listen to
The end of the phrase.
"For the Kingdom of heaven is theirs."
The Beatitude of poverty
Is the anticipated possession of the Kingdom.
Seek this Kingdom,
The "rest" will be given you.
The promised hundredfold
Will flow towards you.
An exchange according to God's measure.
Immeasurable gladness of the poverty of the
                                        Kingdom.
Despoilment—to be sure.
Sacrifice, never.

The poverty of the Kingdom introduces into
another order,

The order of charity.
"It is so good to be poor . . ."
So good only to use the good things of earth
For the coming of the Kingdom
In ourselves and in others.
So good to make them one's servants
Instead of being their slaves.
So good to grow poorer
And to become enriched with living hope,
And with charity.

Repeat it unwearingly, Sister Mary of the Cross.
Repeat it to us.
Repeat it in this our age.
Teach us the gladness of the first Beatitude:
"My little ones,
"It is so good to be poor,
"To have nothing,
"To depend on God
"For everything."

"MY JESUS, I HAVE ONLY YOU . . ."

A very old walnut prie-dieu,
This one or some other,
We don't know.

What we are certain of
Is that on this spot,
Sister Mary of the Cross,
You knelt often.

Little has changed since that time—
The same white stone railing
Of the gallery,
The semi-obscurity of the sanctuary*,
The massive solidity of the pillar of the transept
Hiding you from view.

Here, you appear to us just as a friendly hand
Has sculptured you:
Almost monastic,
With your hands joined,
And your eyelids lowered
Over some secret contemplation.

Some will say—the objection comes easily—

"Is it really Jeanne Jugan?"
They have another image in their mind:
Bending a little under the weight of a basket
That is half covered by your breton mantle,
You are walking,
You are walking, with your eyes firmly fixed on
high,

---

*The large white altar which can be seen in the illustration has been replaced to conform with the new liturgy.

Towards an invisible destination that your gaze
                                          never leaves.
You are walking, drawing into the dynamism
Of your elan
A young companion,
One of your first daughters.

Must we stop with this vision?
Will others show us a third image?
You, still,
But you are no longer alone,
Other faces enframe you:
Aged faces, wrinkled, saddened.
From the serenity of your features,
A rediscovered peace descends on them.
It gives new light to their eyes.
. . . It seems as though you are about to smile
And communicate to us
The joy, so mysterious to us,
So great to you,
Thus to be in the midst of these aged faces.

From these three images

Are we to choose,
Each one according to his temperament?

There is no need to choose.
But . . .
What "but" do you want to offer?
Three different "Jeanne Jugans"?
Not at all.
One only "Jeanne Jugan"
But seen in a new light of Love in each image,
For the features of Love are infinite.
We cannot choose.
The three images make up only one.
They overlay the same reality:
The presence of a great, many-faceted Love.

When one loves little,
Or not at all,
One is immediately satisfied.
Satisfied with one's mediocrity,
Weary of advancing.
One settles down. One no longer moves.

"Jesus is waiting for you in the Chapel. Go and find Him when your strength and patience are giving out, when you feel lonely and helpless. Say to Him:

"You know well what is
happening, my dear Jesus. I
have only You. Come to my
aid . . .
And then go your way. And
don't worry about knowing
how you are going to manage.
It is enough to have told Our
good Lord. He has an excellent
memory."

But you, you press forward.
You will press forward all your life.
Whoever loves can never stand still,
Whoever loves must advance unceasingly,
Further, still further,
Still further again,
Ever further.
Always unsatisfied with one's love.
Always in search of more love.

These aged faces—so numerous in our streets—
Does an unloving heart see them?
Does it even know they exist?
Such a one brushes against them. Happy if he
                        doesn't bump into them.

That's all.
He ignores them. They have no place in his life.
You will never see him in their midst.

This life entwined—exchange and dialogue,
This happiness given and received:
This is Love's success.

And so,

Why join your hands
Instead of continuing to hold them out
To those unloved souls who are crying out for
                                   their warmth?

Why close your eyes?
"Life" for them
Depends, perhaps, on meeting a friendly glance.
Are you going to refuse them this gift?
Are they, on account of you,
Going to lack love?

Our reasoning has taken the wrong path.
Without your joined hands,
Without your lowered eyes,
You would never have pressed forward and
                   opened the way to many others.

Without your praying hands
And the colloquy with God that they signify,
We should not be able to picture you in the midst
                             of these aged faces.

In your life,
All begins and all is completed
With your joined hands

4. Sayings of Jeanne Jugan

And lowered eyes.

The old walnut prie-dieu
Explains everything.

It throws into relief, in the centre of your life,
This presence,
The intimate and continual presence of God;
Generating within you a love that is overflowing,
As well as exclusive.

"My little ones"—you say—
"Refuse God nothing.
"Accustom yourselves to do everything for Him.
". . . Let us love Him very much, that is all that
is necessary.

"He is so good . . .
"Love God very much.
"All for Him,
"Do everything through love."

And, on your lips,
Each of these affirmations is alive,

Already lived,
Taken as they stand,
Bearers of a conviction rooted in the depths of
                                    your being.

Yes, the old walnut prie-dieu explains everything.
On this spot,
Marvellously,
One of the most beautiful promises of the Lord
                              became a reality for you:
"Whoever abides in Me, and I in him,
"Will bear fruit, much fruit."

Here, in the silence of a prayer
That no spiritual diary
Will ever divulge,
You encountered the Lord.
There passed, between Him and you,
And between you and Him,
That interchange of love which defies description.
In Him you saw all things clearly,
True love of neighbour.
Here, more than at any other moment,

You were efficacious and active.

Here, love urged you on your forward march.
It rendered your heart simple,
Your soul peaceful,
Gentle,
Capable of communicating in the joy of the
                                    Cross.

Finally, love unveiled to you its great secret.
The secret which transforms our action into
                            contemplation,

And shows forth in every one of our actions
The radiance of an unceasing Presence.
The continuity of a dialogue
That neither persons,
Nor events
Have power to interrupt.

Kneeling, on this spot,
God made known to you the supreme efficacity,
The final course left,
To the soul that loves.

Who can no longer do anything
—Having already done everything—
But leave all in God's hands.

Free gift of the Lord
—But how worthy of note—
Is a vocation marked with the stamp of human
values
And of supernatural plenitude!

Jeanne Jugan's is of this kind.
She had nothing to do with it.
Her only merit lay in not burying the talent.

Painting of an anonymous artist, dating from 1850, approximately.

Her vocation opens her soul to God
And opens it also to others.

No discord here.
The "second commandment" does not upset her
life,
It gives it its wonderful human balance,
—As objective as it is realistic—
And its supernatural plenitude.
Not the slightest contradiction.
Still less any of those unreal problems which
engulf some people.

On the day when, unable to resist the vision
Of an old woman about to die,
Alone,
In a hovel,
She carries to her own bed
The sightless invalid,
The two lines of Jeanne's vocation,
The human and the divine,
Join together to become one.
It is something completed

As much as something beginning.
There is no turning back.
The hand is put to the plough.
The limits of her little room
Have just exploded, together with those of her
heart.
They have been thrown open to embrace the
world.

Already, by thousands,
And hundreds of thousands,
From every horizon,
Other Aged,
Solitary,
Blind,
Paralysed in body or in soul,
Have joined the one whom, with difficulty,
Up a narrow winding staircase,
She has just carried in her arms
And placed on her bed.

Jeanne must, now, follow through this gesture of
hers to its end.

To the end of her vocation.
To the consummation of authentic compassion.
Not its counterfeit,
Its faked semblance.

The caricature of compassion
Which stoops to . . .
Acts charitably towards . . .
Condescends . . .
Is moved to pity.

True compassion has nothing to do with all that.
To have compassion, is no longer to pay attention
to self.

To be attentive only to others,
And to look on them as one would oneself.
To have compassion, is to accept an active part
In that drama which, since the Incarnation,
Is bringing mankind back to God,
By way of Calvary.

To have compassion, is to suffer with.
To see and accept the other,
Just as he is—even with his sin—
To be open to him, ready to help;
To share unselfishly;
To relieve him of his burden
By taking its weight on one's own shoulders.

Your compassion, Jeanne,

Has become one with the Lord's.
It accepts the Incarnation,
Having taken account of all that this involves,
Believing itself always the receiver.
For it esteems,
Appreciates,
Magnifies.

And so, from the night when the aged Anne
Slept in her bed,
Jeanne belongs to her Lord and to the Elderly of
                                          the human family
By the same bond.
She is at the mercy of them all.
She will no longer separate them.
They may take all from her.
They will take all.

If we doubt this,
See how she lives,
Listen to her.

"—Love God very much,

"So that you can look after the Old People well.
". . . For it is Jesus
"Whom you care for in them."

"Be kind,
"Especially with the infirm . . .
"Love them well . . .
"Oh yes, be kind.
"It is a great grace God is giving you.
"In serving them, it is Himself whom you are
                                           serving."

"Never forget,
"Never forget
"That the poor are Our Lord."

The plenitude of your vocation resides,
Sister Mary of the Cross,
In the constant flow
From the human to the divine,
From your Aged brothers
To your eternal Lord.

Could we still speak of anything merely of this
                                    world in your life,
Of common tasks, or lowly?

When, with so much ease,
You stamp the divine on human actions,
And vice versa.

God gave you love
For those who are sorrowfully ending
Their earthly journey;
Those whom, already, He sees arriving
On the threshold of His Home.
It is a mandate.
In the eyes of the Church.
In the eyes of the world.

It is for you to convey to them,
To interpret for them in everyday life,
The tenderness, the kindness of God,
The affection God has for them, his Eldest

Children.

You have to bring this tenderness
Within their grasp,
So that they may take hold of it,
Feel it,
Know it for what it is, in all truth,
And that it has a name: happiness,

Even here-below.

But man does not live by bread alone,
By things of this earth.
The soul's hunger tortures, as does that of the
*   body.*

It is deadly also.
The tragedy is that it passes unnoticed.
Those who are dying of bodily hunger
Have a chance of meeting a Good Samaritan,
But what of those who are dying from the hunger
*   of the soul?*
Your mandate of love compels you even in this:
"Knock. Knock at the gate of Heaven
"For souls."

You insist, thus letting us feel how this hunger
*   for souls*

Gnaws at you:
"Knock, knock . . ."
To those who are dying of bodily hunger
A soothing act of kindness suffices.
To the others, an unrestricted gift is necessary
—Renewed at each instant—
The only kind that redeems and transforms,

"THE HAIL MARY WILL TAKE US TO HEAVEN . . ."

"The Hail Mary will take us to Heaven."
Nothing more simple.
Why do we always complicate life?
God loves simplicity.

"The Hail Mary will take us to Heaven."
What a good meditation we could make

Let us say a Hail Mary together."

Sister Mary of the Cross's usual way of saying Thank you.

On this slogan—pardon the expression—
Sister Mary of the Cross!
It has been said that whenever you spoke of Mary,
You had "an air of Paradise".
And that the only object you clung to
Was your poor rosary.

—In your younger years, it was your travelling
companion.

—In old age, you loved to recite it with the
novices.
In your comings and goings,
You fingered it continuously.
And around it your hands
Were clasped for the last time,
Forever.

You show it to us as if to say:

How very mistaken they are who think God is
Goodness knows where,
Far away, hidden.
And very mistaken too, folks who imagine
Heaven can be gained
After astronautic feats of valor

◄ Fragments of the Rosary beads of Sister Mary of the Cross,
discovered at her exhumation in 1936.

Or years of theology!
To reach God, and with Him Paradise:
Is child's play.

Mind the word: child's play.
To be a child.
If we are children, we need a mother.
Now you have understood:
"The Hail Mary will take us to Heaven."
The path is well marked out.
God gave us Our Lady for this purpose.
Expressly.
Mother, Teacher, Guide,
Leader: Gate of Heaven.
She lacks nothing. She has everything.
Everything, I tell you!

The defects are on our side.
"My children, you love Our Lady?
"She will be your Mother!"
She can be our mother in the measure that we
                                    love her.
Try, try as you may your whole life long,
You will never exhaust the treasures of her
                                    maternity.

You can see how this is the right path,
The straight path leading to Paradise.

"My children, you love Our Lady,
"She will be your Mother!"

Go ahead, slip your hand in hers,
Say to her: "Never let me go."
You are entering on the most wonderful
adventure in the world,
That of the Redemption.
The adventure where he who loses, wins.
The adventure of a life completely given.
Of blood shed. That of the soul.
Unknown to all, save God.

When you will see the gate of Heaven about to
open,
You will only have to say to Her:
"You know you are my Mother."
You will have won in this adventure of the
Redemption,
Won for yourself and for many others
For all eternity.

*Her special characteristic was the praise
and admiration of God; her joy in speaking of His benefits, and of the maternal
care of Providence. Neither setbacks nor
success ever interrupted her "Bene-
dicamus Domino". She was for ever
praising God.*

Witness of a native of
Saint-Servan concerning
Jeanne Jugan.

She was for ever praising God . . .

*Though so many, the witnesses always agree.
In times of setback, in times of joy,
They repeat the same phrase,
That rings out like a refrain:*

"Blessed be God!"

"We must always say: Blessed be God.
"Thank you, my God.
"Or, glory be to God!"
"He is so good, God".

She was for ever praising God . . .

With you, Sister Mary of the Cross, everything is
cause for praise.
For you, everything bears a divine imprint:
Creation, events,
The instruments God makes use of . . . good or
bad;
The extraordinary expansion of the Work
For which He made you His own.
The miracle of Providence, daily renewed.

Providence . . .
The infinite tenderness of the Heart of God
Revealed tangibly,
Continuously.
Ever since you gave yourself up to it,
You have never regretted this abandon,
This dependence on the Lord.

Failure, success, cannot harm it.
By it, one is rooted in the Will of God.
It transforms everything into charity.
And so your soul would contemplate its Lord
In everything.
That is why it exults.
In the background of every least event,
In filigree behind creatures,
God stands.
You no longer see anything but Him.

We are not making this up: you admitted as
                              much yourself:

"When you will be old
"You will no longer see anything . . .
"As for me, I no longer see anything but God . . ."

The years slip by at the same tempo for all of us.
Time does its work.
It separates. It purifies.
It does not divinise.
Beyond the passing years
The real vision of God
Remains the personal conquest, long and patient,

Of each one's love.
Happy are you, Sister Mary of the Cross
To have reached the summit!

"As for me, I no longer see anything but God."

Fatigue, infirmities, suffering,
Pass under His divine Gaze
Before reaching your soul.
There, even they become praise.
To others, they are a burden. To you, they are a
                                                            joy.

To the leaven of old age,
They substitute tokens of eternity:
A wonderful youthfulness of heart.
Fresh as Spring,
With new resources, unwavering hope,
Joy that communicates itself to others.

"Blessed be God!
"We must say, always:
"Blessed be God,
"Thank you, my God
"Or: Glory be to God."

"Eternal Father, open your
gates today to the most
miserable of your children,
but one who greatly longs to
see you . . .

O Mary, my dear mother,
come to me. You know that
I love you and that I long
to see you."

The very last words of Sister Mary of the Cross.

LE DIVIN MODÈLE.

d'un
ie de
sées et
saintes

te Vierge
ouvrage,
acer selon
On n'a
s nombreux
s livres, soit
em, à saint
t à quelques
templatifs; ils
onnes qui n'en-
; et ceux qui la
ésirent, les con-
st donc borné à
qui ont paru su-
, à redresser des
cer des expressions
essions plus énergi-
les négligences de

CONTENTS

✝

Photos: **FORTIER**

T. PICARRI, O.P. (Prie-dieu)

BUCKINGHAM (Wash. D.C.) (Bronze)

Frontispiece: Sculptor—**Fr. Marie Bernard, O.C.R.**

Printed by the *Daughters of St. Paul*
50 St. Paul's Avenue, Jamaica Plain,
Boston, Mass. 02130